Post-Traumatic Growth

Overcoming Trauma with Resilience and Purpose

Table of Contents

Chapter 1. Introduction

Experience and adversity may sometimes seem like insurmountable challenges, imparting profound, perhaps even shattering effects on one's psyche. Yet, there exists a hidden jewel within such adversity — an empowering facet referred to as Post-Traumatic Growth (PTG). This Special Report delves into the gratifying world of PTG, elucidating how trauma survivors can marshal resilience and assign purpose to their lives. Rather than employing jargon or technical terms, the report is written in a widely accessible language, providing deeply informative, yet easy-to-digest insights. Unfurling a kaleidoscope of hope within the aftermath of distress, the report offers readers valuable knowledge on harnessing personal hardships with an empowering perspective. By exploring this groundbreaking Special Report, prepare to be inspired and motivated to transcend your trials and tribulations and reframe them into stepping stones toward growth, resilience, and ultimately, a transformational rebirth.

Chapter 2. Understanding Trauma: The Initial Shock

Human beings, much like the world we live in, are inherently complex and multifaceted. Replete with diverse emotions, experiences, and perspectives, we are a compelling amalgam of resilience and vulnerability. One of the most deeply affecting experiences that can irrevocably alter the course of an individual's life is trauma. It can manifest as an emotional response to a deeply disturbing or distressing event that overwhelms an individual's capacity to cope, often eliciting feelings of helplessness and effacing their sense of self and security.

2.1. The Concept of Trauma

First, let's lay the groundwork by understanding what trauma truly entails. It's not a mere reaction to a stressful event but signifies much more. An event, situation, or experience can be deemed traumatic when it's so distressing or disturbing that it eclipses your ability to cope. Any happenstance that threatens or breaches the sanctity of your basic human needs – like safety, love, respect, and autonomy – can germinate the seeds of trauma.

Trauma can stem from varied sources, including such severe situations like war, rape, natural disasters, accidents, or child abuse. However, it's vital to recognize that not all individuals respond to the same event in an identical manner. What might be traumatic for one may not lead to similar repercussions for another. This is primarily due to individuals' unique abilities to cope, their previous life experiences, and the support they receive post the event. Hence, even seemingly 'lesser' instances of neglect, humiliation, persistent stress, or sudden upheaval can also precipitate trauma.

2.2. The Response to Trauma: Initial Shock

The immediate response to a traumatic event typically manifests as a whirlwind of chaotic emotions, referred to as the initial shock. This shock arises out of an intense struggle to reconcile with the new, alarming reality - a reality characterized by a harrowing ordeal that defies your prior understanding of the world, thereby fracturing your sense of safety.

Gravity of the event and your proximity to it, both physically and emotionally, largely dictate your response. Initial shock generally oscillates between states of disbelief, fear, sadness, and even numbness. Feelings can be stormy, blinding you with their intensity, or you may encounter an emotional void, where you're girdled by apathy and disconnectedness.

Many might experience physical symptoms mirroring their emotional upheaval – a racing heartbeat, churning stomach, trembling hands – a primitive response from the body as it preps for 'fight or flight.' Some might also grapple with mental discord like difficulty in concentration, distorted memory of the event or continual replaying of the trauma.

2.3. Numbness and Denial: An Adaptive Response

In the immediate aftermath of a traumatic event, a common response is numbness or denial. This act of shutting down or blocking out the emotional experience is a protective mechanism – the mind's chivalrous attempt to shield you from a reality that's too brutal to bear.

Such a response might prompt onlookers to perceive you as 'strong' or 'unaffected.' However, beneath this apparent calm, often lurks a chaotic emotional storm that's temporarily been silenced but not alleviated. It is, with time and therapeutic intervention, that these suppressed feelings unfurl and can thus be addressed.

2.4. The Evolution of Shock: Post-Traumatic Stress

With time, the shock might simmer and possibly transmute into Post-Traumatic Stress Disorder (PTSD), especially if the initial response wasn't sufficiently managed. This involves persistent re-experiencing of the traumatic event, avoidance of anything resembling it, augmented arousal, as well as cognitive and mood changes.

The prospect of trauma might appear overwhelming, gloomy, even damning. Yet, this is only a partial representation of the entire narrative. Human beings are remarkably resilient, often rising from the ashes of their devastating experiences, a reality we explore as the report unfolds.

As we delve deeper into the aftermath of trauma, we'll discern the mosaic of multifarious responses that make the topic of trauma such a complex yet intriguing one. We will also commence our journey towards recognizing and understanding the profound mechanism of Post-Traumatic Growth, wherein seeds of profound transformation are often sown in the heart-rending soil of trauma.

Chapter 3. Resilience: The Human Spirit's Shield

Resilience isn't merely about bouncing back from adversity; it's about showing up, even when the stakes are high and the challenges immense. Humans have struggled and thrived for thousands of years, not because they've escaped hardship, but because they've learned to weather it, to adapt and prevail. It is this tenacity that scaffolds the human spirit, enabling us to grow despite — and sometimes due to — adversities. And at the heart of it all is the inherent human capacity to keep forging forward, to look adversity in the eye, and say, "I will not be defeated. I will grow from this."

3.1. The Concept of Resilience

Resilience, as a concept, is multidimensional and intricate, encompassing a variety of psychological, sociological, and biological factors. Broadly, it can be defined as the human ability to adapt in the face of trauma, adversity, or stress. It's no magic pill that vanishes problems away; instead, it's a bundle of thoughts, actions, and strategies that can be tailored to confront every unique hurdle that life throws at us.

The punctuated episodes of resilience that humans display are trifurcated — instantaneous, gradual, and sporadic. Instantaneous resilience springs into action at the moment of adversity, while gradual resilience takes root over time, building resistance piece by piece. Sporadic resilience is inconsistent, flitting in and out as life's disruptions wax and wane. Regardless of its form, the prism of resilience provides a beacon of hope amid distress.

3.2. Resilience and Post-Traumatic Growth

Resilience plays a crucial role in fostering Post-Traumatic Growth. When we speak of PTG, we talk about an individual's capacity to harness pain and adversity, to utilize the ravages of trauma as fertile ground for personal evolution. This process isn't just about survival — resilience morphs into a transformative power, enabling survivors of hardship to mold a more profound and meaningful existence post-trauma.

Resilience fuels PTG by creating a framework for trauma processing, lending a perspective that validates pain and stimulates healing. As individuals harness their resilience, they gradually move from shock and disbelief to acceptance and growth. They learn to perceive adversities not as impervious walls but as obstacles to overcome and grow from.

3.3. Building Resilience: A Spectrum of Strategies

Building resilience isn't a one-size-fits-all endeavor. Each individual has a unique configuration of strengths, coping mechanisms, and contextual realities. The journey towards resilience involves identifying and strengthening these faculties, and may incorporate a spectrum of strategies.

1. **Optimism**: Approaching life with a positive outlook can render adversities manageable. By focusing on the possible and embracing the unknown, optimism can elevate resilience.

2. **Self-care**: Taking care of physical health aids emotional resilience. By ensuring regular exercise, a balanced diet, enough sleep, and recreation, individuals can better tackle hardships.

3. **Connection**: Building strong, supportive relationships provides reassurance and assistance in challenging times, thereby strengthening resilience.

4. **Mental agility**: Cultivating a flexible mindset can assist in adapting to change, an essential facet of resilience.

5. **Purpose**: Identifying a compelling reason to persevere adds fuel to resilience. Whether it's a goal, dream, or duty to others, purpose can critically motivate persistence amid adversity.

3.4. Resilience: A Lifelong Path

Resilience isn't an endpoint but a journey, a winding path sown with challenges and triumphs alike. It does not mean immunity to pain, but the capacity to keep progressing despite it. The path of resilience might be rugged and steep, but the vistas it offers — of strength, healing, and growth — make the journey not only worthwhile but truly transformative.

Ultimately, resilience acts as the human spirit's shield, bolstering us against trauma's brute force, and allowing growth to blossom from the ashes of adversity. It's a potent symbol of human tenacity, a testament to the extraordinary capabilities we embody, and inspire us to acknowledge, elevate, and embrace our resilient nature.

Remember, resilience isn't about having no cracks — it's about letting the light seep in through those very cracks and illuminating the path to post-traumatic growth. It's about viewing those fissures not as scars of defeat, but as badges of survival and marks of incredible strength. Hence, as we unlock these sections about post-traumatic growth, we embark on a journey — a voyage that acknowledges the courage to face adversity, the strength to survive it, and the wisdom to grow from it.

Chapter 4. Defining Post-Traumatic Growth: The Silver Lining

Life has an uncanny knack for throwing curveballs. Unpredictable and often capricious, it presents an eclectic blend of experiences ranging from the euphoria of triumphs to the distress of adversities. These adversities, especially the traumatic ones, leave behind deep-seated effects on our psyche, frequently triggering responses such as Post-Traumatic Stress Disorder (PTSD). Less known, but equally potent, is the phenomenon that can unfurl in the wake of such traumatic incidences — Post-Traumatic Growth (PTG).

4.1. Understanding Post-Traumatic Growth

Post-Traumatic Growth is not, as some might assume, merely bouncing back to your initial mental state prior to trauma, a concept otherwise referred to as resilience. Instead, PTG is about achieving a state of well-being that extends beyond your prior level of functioning, wherein you perceive benefits from your struggle with challenging experiences. This progressive transformation following trauma can mold you into a stronger, more mature, and more fulfilled individual than before.

While trauma can significantly disrupt your life, it is essential to understand that growth simultaneously happens. People affected by various traumatic conditions, such as severe medical illness, loss of loved ones, accidents, natural disasters, violence, or war, can concurrently experience PTG. This potential for growth does not negate the pain inflicted by trauma; instead, it is posited that trauma provides fertile ground for such growth to occur.

4.2. The Origins of Post-Traumatic Growth

PTG is an intricate construct of human psychology that arose from the shadows of the more well-known PTSD. Richard Tedeschi and Lawrence Calhoun, psychologists from the University of North Carolina, were among the earliest researchers in the field of PTG. In the 1990's they began to explore the transformative positives that some trauma survivors experienced amidst their suffering.

Their research shed light on the powerful consonance residing within the heartache. They discovered that alongside the most catastrophic upheavals of human experience were paradoxically juxtaposed moments of profound insight, intense self-awareness, and an unparalleled capacity for empathy. Therein lay the germination of the concept of PTG, a phenomenon of growth flourishing in the rubble of distress.

4.3. The Key Components of Post-Traumatic Growth

Tedeschi and Calhoun identified five key areas where post-traumatic growth generally manifests:

1. *Improved Relationships*: Trauma survivors often express a sense of increased compassion and intimacy in their relationships. They cultivate an enhanced appreciation for others, especially those with similar hardships.

2. *Identification of New Possibilities*: Trauma can unfetter individuals from previous life paths and prompt them to discover unanticipated avenues in life.

3. *Increased Personal Strength*: Trauma survivors frequently find within themselves a reservoir of strength they hadn't noticed

before, allowing a newfound confidence in their resilience.

4. *Spiritual Change*: These experiences could lead to a profound shift in spiritual beliefs or, for others, strengthen pre-existing spiritual foundations.

5. *Greater Appreciation of Life*: A heightened appreciation for life and a changed sense of priorities are often observed in trauma survivors.

4.4. Embracing Post-Traumatic Growth

Embracing PTG involves acceptance, patience, and a willingness to grapple with the discomfort that the journey of growth entails. This process necessitates that you confront the trauma, regurgitate the distress it caused, and then gradually embark on a metamorphic journey to discover a newfound sense of self.

As idiosyncratic as human experiences are, so too is the experience of PTG. It's significant to underline that PTG is not a guaranteed outcome from trauma, nor is it insinuated that trauma is a prerequisite for personal growth. PTG is simply a beacon of hope extending beyond the agony, guiding survivors to the discovery of hidden strengths and a renewed sense of life purpose.

4.5. Facilitating Post-Traumatic Growth

Given the crucial importance of contextual and individual factors in influencing the course of PTG, it is essential to approach the pursuit of growth with a tailored strategy that suits one's needs and circumstances. Psychotherapy and counseling hold considerable promise in this regard, providing a safe environment for trauma survivors to express and process their feelings.

In addition to therapy, self-help strategies, such as writing about one's experience, maintaining a gratitude journal, mindfulness practice, maintaining a healthy lifestyle, and seeking social support, can also facilitate post-traumatic growth. The interplay of therapeutic intervention and these self-help strategies can significantly enhance the process of PTG, allowing one to navigate their trauma and seek meaning amidst turmoil.

To conclude, PTG is not about glossing over trauma or denying its devastating consequences. It is about recognizing that alongside the daunting adversities, there exists a silver lining; a lining that can guide us towards renewed resilience and personal growth. The bitter wisdom garnered through trauma could indeed catalyze a transformation—our very own Phoenix rising from the ashes. Let us thus engage intimately with the potential of PTG and gear ourselves for this transformational journey that celebrates the full spectrum of human experience.

Chapter 5. Key Aspects of Post-Traumatic Growth

Adversity is an uninvited guest that mysteriously finds its way into our lives, effecting unforeseen changes. These changes can be traumatic, leaving us feeling lost and desolate in their wake. On the otherhand, adversity can also catalyze a transformative process known as Post-Traumatic Growth, where individuals emerge stronger, wiser, and profoundly altered in positive ways.

5.1. Recognizing the Potential for Growth

It may seem paradoxical to consider growth and positive change stemming from adversity and trauma. Still, numerous studies have identified five key aspects of Post-Traumatic Growth: new possibilities, personal strength, spiritual change, relating to others, and appreciation of life. These crucial points are not solely the result of multi-tiered human resilience but also a testament to the inherently adaptive nature of human beings.

(1) New Possibilities: Trauma can alter the trajectory of an individual's life path. When people endure devastating occurrences, they may feel as if their life script has been ripped to shreds. However, this decimation of the 'known' can unexpectedly open up new possibilities, igniting a latent sense of adventure, instigating change in career paths, hobbies or personal goals.

(2) Personal Strength: Surviving a traumatic event can induce in the individual a newfound realization of their capacities. This awareness of having weathered a profound storm often translates into strong self-belief and confidence. Although the validation springs from adversity, it can empower individuals to face future tribulations with

unruffled courage.

(3) Spiritual Change: Many times, trauma can catalyze a spiritual evolution. This may be expressed as a renewed belief in religion or a heightened sense of spiritual connectivity. Sometimes, such spiritual re-awakening allows individuals to find solace and comfort, thereby fostering their recovery and growth.

(4) Relating to Others: Post-Traumatic Growth can enhance empathy, making it easier to connect emotionally with others. Survivors may find that their experiences enable them to relate to others in distress, thereby imbuing their relationships with depth and richness.

(5) Appreciation of Life: A brush with adversity can magnify the significance of life's simple pleasures. Trauma survivors often speak of a newfound appreciation for life, where they not just exist, but live — appreciating and celebrating each moment.

5.2. The Process of Post-Traumatic Growth

Understanding the intricacies of Post-Traumatic Growth involves looking at the process it requires. It starts with the experience of trauma, disrupting our previously held beliefs and expectations about life and ourselves. Such a shift in worldview is not instant; it's a process that evolves over time.

This evolution is empowered by resilience, a characteristic inherent in all individuals. Resilience is not a static trait one either possesses or lacks, but rather a dynamic process that fluctuates over time, primarily fueled by one's perceptions, responses, and reactions to life events.

To foster post-traumatic growth, one needs to undertake cognitive processing, a necessity in assimilating the adverse experience into one's life narrative. This processing involves challenging and restructuring formerly held beliefs and assumptions in the face of new reality, leading to cognitive balance.

One essential part of this process includes narrative development, where people begin to piece together and articulate the impacts of trauma on their lives. The act of telling one's story allows for the construction of a trauma narrative, and in doing so, individuals can start to make sense of their experience.

Likewise, social support is a potent catalyst for Post-Traumatic Growth. Positive and supportive relationships can help individuals create a nurturing environment where growth can develop.

5.3. From Survivor to Thriver

Transitioning from merely surviving to thriving is a profound shift that occurs during Post-Traumatic Growth. Survivors do more than merely exist post-trauma; they show us how to transform our darkest moments into catalysts for growth and profound change.

In conclusion, the journey through adversity is undeniably a challenging one. Yet, the path doesn't end at survival; it has the potential to lead to Post-Traumatic Growth. A strength emerges through the cracks of brokenness, highlighting that it's possible for individuals not only to bounce back but also to bounce forward towards a strengthened, more resilient self. Though daunting, understanding and embarking on the journey of Post-Traumatic Growth can transform adversity from an overwhelming specter into a wellspring of growth, resilience, and rebirth.

Chapter 6. The Role of Social Support in Facilitating Growth

Navigating through the aftermath of a traumatic event often necessitates a robust support system – a network of trusted individuals who provide emotional, instrumental or informational support. Such social support often serves as the catalyst to the process of Post-Traumatic Growth.

6.1. The Importance of Social Support

Social support networks are the bedrock of post-trauma recovery. While the individual trauma survivor grapples with unexpected life changes, the ones around them can nurture their resilience. Comprehensive support networks provide a buffer against traumatic stress and mitigate the risk of developing post-traumatic stress disorder (PTSD). They offer emotional comfort and assurance, improve the survivor's self-esteem, and foster a sense of belonging while navigating the stormy seas of adversity.

Conversely, lack of social support can exacerbate feelings of isolation, abandonment, loneliness, which in turn can increase the likelihood of depression and anxiety, and impede the recovery process. Yet, it is essential to recognize that the quality of support matters more than the quantity. A handful of supportive relationships can be more significant in facilitating PTG than a larger network of relatively indifferent ones.

6.2. Types of Social Support

To understand the role of social support fully, it is crucial to identify its types. Primarily, it segregates into four types: emotional, instrumental (or tangible), informational, and appraisal support.

- Emotional support refers to actions that make others feel loved and cared for. It includes empathy, concern, love, trust, and a listening ear.

- Instrumental support refers to substantial aid, like financial assistance, provision of material resources, or aid with various tasks.

- Informational support involves provision of advice, suggestions, and information that a person can use to address problems.

- Appraisal support involves the provision of information that is useful for self-evaluation purposes; for instance, constructive feedback, affirmation, and social comparison.

Each of these types plays a critical role in successful recovery and inducing PTG. For example, emotional support can help a survivor process their emotions in a healthy and non-judgmental environment, instrumental support can lighten their daily burdens, informational support can guide them towards effective coping mechanisms, and appraisal support can aid in re-evaluating their self-perception in a positive way.

6.3. How Social Support Facilitates Growth

Social support primarily facilitates growth in three significant ways: fostering positive psychology, encouraging active coping strategies, and reconstructing narrative around trauma.

Positive psychology, with its focus on strengths, virtues, and nurturing what is best within us, can act as vehicle for healing. Research shows that social support encourages positivity in survivors, helping elevate feelings of self-efficacy, optimism, and self-esteem, while simultaneously reducing feelings of guilt, shame, and isolation.

Active coping strategies are a key component in the process of PTG. But learning them can be challenging. Here, social support can play an instrumental role by modelling resilience and providing practical tips. This can boost a survivor's adaptive coping skills, paving way for a determined grappling with trauma and fostering their growth.

Finally, reconstructing the narrative around trauma is a key aspect of PTG. This involves changing the perspective from being a "victim" to a "survivor" and finding personal strength within the fabric of struggle. Social support can help in navigating this perspective shift, as shared experiences or insights can help the survivor re-articulate their story in a more empowering light.

6.4. Roadblocks and Solutions in Accessing Social Support

However, utilizing social support after trauma can come with unique challenges. Fear of judgement, isolation, and lack of understanding from others may prevent survivors from seeking help. However, these roadblocks can be subdued by raising awareness, promoting empathy, and fostering an overall supportive atmosphere in society.

Moreover, depending on their comfort, survivors might find it easier to reach out to professional support systems, like psychiatrists, psychologists, or support groups, instead of or in conjunction with, personal networks. Digital platforms also offer appealing alternatives, including online forums and helplines, providing anonymity and a sense of safety.

In conclusion, an unperturbed vessel of social support becomes a beacon of hope for trauma survivors, guiding them through tumultuous waters towards the land of recovery and growth. Critically, we all ought to do our part in amplifying its power and making it more accessible to all individuals we can reach. If we each foster one thread of the social support web, it can expand vastly to envelope all those grappling under the arduous trials of life. Together, we can ensure that adversity becomes an avenue for growth, resilience and transformative rebirth.

Chapter 7. Therapeutic Approaches to Enhance Growth

It is a long-established fact that professional therapeutic approaches play a crucial role in aiding those affected by trauma to navigate their path towards healing. However, it is equally important to recognize that therapeutic counseling can also instigate and foster Post-Traumatic Growth (PTG). It is not just about aiding survivors to retread towards normalcy, but about enabling them to discover an enriched view of life after experiencing trauma.

7.1. Cognitive-Behavioral Therapy

Cognitive-Behavioral Therapy (CBT) corresponds to a highly effective and prevalent approach. Built on the idea that our thoughts, feelings, and behaviors are interwoven, CBT aims to modify thought patterns that result in harmful behaviors and emotional distress.

Through regular sessions, the counselor meticulously guides the individual to identify cognitive distortions that contribute to emotional distress. By challenging these distorted thoughts and promoting healthier alternatives, individuals can begin to perceive their trauma differently, potentially setting the groundwork for PTG.

For instance, if an individual adopts the thought, *"this horrific event has ruined my life,"* it is the task of the therapist to render the thought alternative like *"the event was horrendous, but it is also an opportunity for me to reassess life priorities and grow."* Once the trauma survivor can integrate such transformative thoughts, this can pave the way for positive change.

7.2. Narrative Exposure Therapy

Narrative Exposure Therapy (NET), a unique form of trauma-focused CBT, has proven especially useful when dealing with individuals grappling with recurring traumatic thoughts and challenging life situations. NET assists survivors in reconstructing the chronological narrative of their traumatic experience.

The therapist employs this technique to draw out the vivid detail of their experience, hears their story, and subtly guides the person to psychologically revisit the traumatic event. Consequently, this helps to diminish the overwhelming impact of the traumatic memory and the emotional distress attached to the same. Also, through the narrative, the person can identify their resilience and strength displayed during adversity, laying a foundation for PTG.

7.3. Mindfulness-based Therapy

Mindfulness-based Therapy (MBT), grounded in the fundamental practice of mindfulness, encourages individuals to intentionally focus their attention on the present moment without judgement.

The basis of MBT—displaying awareness, kindness and acceptance towards thoughts and feelings—even those that may be distressing—can be instrumental in overcoming traumatic stress. Once the individuals are equipped to manage their emotional responses, they often find it easier to find positive aspects in their life experiences, thus, propelling them toward PTG.

Sessions involving activities, such as mindfulness-based stress reduction, mindfulness-based cognitive therapy, and yoga, help survivors learn to meditate, manage their breathing, or execute certain postures to enhance their sense of well-being.

7.4. Group Therapy

Group therapy sessions serve as cohesive platforms where survivors share experiences and learn from each other. Encapsulating a sense of commonality and belonging, group therapy can conceivably induce PTG, as survivors realize they are not alone and that they can transform their adversity into a story of resilience and strength.

The therapist facilitates discussions in groups, allowing members to express their feelings honestly. The shared experiences can offer much-needed validation, thereby removing feelings of isolation or guilt. Growth happens when survivors witness others who have managed to transform their trauma and draw strength and inspiration from them.

7.5. Positive Psychology Interventions

Positive psychology reflects an approach that underscores the strengths individuals possess to improve their quality of life. By focusing on positive emotions, strengths, and values, therapists seek to cultivate a resilient mindset among survivors, ideally breeding fertile ground for PTG to take root.

Counselors might encourage survivors to engage in a series of activities like maintaining gratitude journals or practicing altruistic actions. These practices often present an alternative outlook, shifting focus from the past traumatic event to the positive aspects of one's life, thus fostering PTG.

7.6. Pharmacotherapy

While the majority of PTG is encapsulated within various therapy forms, the benefits of pharmacotherapy to manage severe symptoms of Post-Traumatic Stress Disorder should not be overlooked. Medications often moderate overwhelming emotional reactions, making it easier for survivors to participate in therapy. As they gain more control over their reactions, the space for positive growth becomes abundant.

In conclusion, the role of therapeutic approaches in stimulating PTG offers a promising route towards healing and growing from trauma. By integrating targeted therapies into treatment programs, survivors can navigate beyond merely coping, evolving onto a path where growth from adversity has the potential to provide them with value and newfound purpose.

Chapter 8. Personal Stories of Growth: Inspirations from Real-life Heroes

Witnessing lives shattered by adversity and chaos, yet emerging stronger and painstakingly stitching together a new reality composed of insight, growth, and profound resilience, is nothing short of inspirational. In the indomitable spirit of such individuals, we find an invigorating energy that fuels our journey to understand personal Post-Traumatic Growth (PTG).

Here, we offer a prismatic view into the world of individuals who have weathered remarkably harsh conditions and come out the other side poised, not merely to survive, but to thrive.

8.1. The Firefighter's Seismic Shift

When 35-year-old Matthew was trapped after a building collapsed while he was attempting a rescue during a fire, he experienced an imminent brush with death. Despite months of physical damage control in hospitals and long-lasting emotional scars, Matthew perceived his experience not as calamity, but as an opportunity to grow. Today, he is an advocate for mental health among first responders, employing his painful memories as teaching tools, turning his adversity into a form of empowerment. His story is a beacon of resilience, showing us that a personal disaster can sometimes clear the path to a more meaningful life.

8.2. Transforming Trauma into Triumph: A Soldier's Story

War-torn landscapes and the disquiet of death triggered a Post-Traumatic Stress Disorder (PTSD) diagnosis for Adam, a decorated army veteran. However, a realization became his turning point: Adam knew he could either be restricted by his diagnosis or use it as a springboard toward growth. Choosing the latter, he started counseling fellow veterans, offering them a place to share their stories without judgment. Through his struggle, he found a purpose, demonstrating that even the deepest trauma can seed the most vibrant growth.

8.3. Rise of a Phoenix: A Domestic Abuse Survivor's Journey

For years, Maria was locked in a cycle of domestic abuse, her existence clouded by psychological harm. The darkness lifted when she finally walked away from her abuser, shook off the shackles of torment, and decided to rise from the ashes. Today, Maria channels her experience into her work as a social worker, assisting others trapped in similar circumstances. The pain she survived fuels her dedication to helping others conquer their adversities. Maria's life exemplifies how PTG can imbue the tormented with strength and passionate purpose.

8.4. Celebrating Scars: A Cancer Warrior's Tale

When Susan was diagnosed with breast cancer, it felt like a death sentence. But overcoming the fear and sorrow brought about a deeper understanding of life. The disease met its match in her resolve, which emerged stronger with each passing therapy session. Now a cancer-free advocate, Susan uses her journey to inspire other cancer patients, reassuring them that disease is not the end, but could be a catalyst for a renewed appreciation for life. Her story is a testament to how traumatic events can forge an unbreakable will.

These real-life instances of PTG are not about celebrating adversity but rather about appreciating the growth opportunities such events can offer. Instead of being mired in their past, these heroes reframe their narratives, deriving strength from their experiences and transforming themselves in the process.

The common thread amongst these stories is the profound human ability to rise from the ashes of disaster, like a Phoenix, committed to living with renewed purpose. Through PTG, individuals can turns their traumas into stepping stones, ultimately fostering a transformative rebirth.

Chapter 9. Infusing Purpose: Rediscovering Meaning after Trauma

Surviving trauma is an arduous and commendable feat in its own right. The scars it leaves behind are indelible marks of life's bruising turns. Paradoxically, the profound lasting effects of trauma can pave the way for a remarkable kind of growth and self-discovery. This is where the beauty of infusing purpose post-trauma surfaces.

9.1. Unveiling the Concept of Purpose

The concept of purpose is as alluring as it is elusive. Yet, its impacts are not just significant but transformative. Purpose is the fulcrum upon which the scale of life tilts, pulling us back when external events threaten to throw us off balance. It is the driving force propelling us to rise every morning, inspiring us to envision a better tomorrow. It gives meaning and direction to life, keeping us engaged and motivated, even when circumstances are painstakingly harsh.

Understanding and nurturing one's purpose in life holds transformative potential, especially for individuals who have braved the storm of trauma. These souls have witnessed the darker shades of existence, and they are the ones who can appreciate the dawn of hope and a renewed purpose most profoundly. Importantly, the task of finding purpose does not deny the pain of trauma but transforms it into a powerful, life-affirming force.

9.2. Steps Toward Finding Purpose

Identifying your purpose following a trauma can be a gradual and deeply personal journey. Here are some starting steps that can guide you on this path.

1. Exploration: Spend time with yourself. Reflect on what matters to you, what makes your heart sing, your beliefs, your values. Dive deep into your desires and passions. Understand what drives you beyond the mundane tasks of everyday life.

2. Connection: Humans are social beings, and we often find meaning through our relationships with others. Connect with people who share similar beliefs, passions, or those who have also experienced a problem that you feel passionate about addressing.

3. Contribution: Consider how you want to make a difference. It could be something personal, like improving your relationship with a loved one, or community-level, like starting a non-profit organization or volunteering your time for a cause you truly care about.

4. Resilience: Sometimes, the path to a greater purpose can be riddled with obstacles. But resilience is the key. It's about forging forward, despite hardships, to find your purpose.

9.3. Role of Resilience in Finding Purpose

Resilience is an instrumental tool in the toolkit of purpose discovery and cultivation. It paves the way for a reclaimed sense of self and a deeper understanding of our strengths and weaknesses. Sturdy mental fortitude is imperative for absorbing the seismic shocks of life, sustaining scratches but avoiding complete wreckage.

Resilient individuals don't just 'bounce back' after a setback; they 'bounce forward.' They adjust their sails amidst the tempest, becoming better navigators of the tumultuous seas of life. They consider each trial an opportunity to accentuate their strengths and address their weaknesses.

Remember, resilience isn't innately a part of us; it is predominantly a learned behavior. It might require the will to face one's own vulnerabilities, and the courage to dissect and understand them, turning them into sources of strength.

9.4. The Symbiotic Relationship between Purpose and Resilience

There exists a fascinating interplay between purpose and resilience. On the one hand, purpose serves as a beacon guiding the ship of resilience amidst foggy adversity. On the other hand, resilience fosters the fortitude to explore, define, and persevere with our purpose.

A clear purpose works as a catalyst in triggering resilience. When adversity strikes, it can fog your vision and lead you astray. But purpose acts like a lighthouse, providing direction and enabling you to keep moving forward. It empowers you to cross the bridge between trauma and transformation, converting your traumatic experiences into stepping stones for growth and healing.

At the same time, resilience galvanizes purpose. Life is often a rollercoaster of aspirations and disappointments. Not every purposeful pursuit concludes successfully, but that's where resilience steps in. It underpins your determination, enhancing your capacity to endure setbacks and try again, thereby ensuring you stay true to your purpose, no matter the hurdles.

9.5. Conclusion: Embracing Purpose in the Wake of Trauma

Trauma may shatter your world and scatter the pieces around you. But within these fragments, you can find the materials to build a new masterpiece. It's about consciously picking up each piece — different from before, yet usable — to erect a transformed existence infused with renewed purpose. Finding purpose after trauma is about understanding that when one chapter of life closes abruptly, another waits to be written with greater wisdom and courage.

Remember, your trauma does not define you; how you respond to it does. So, look at it not as a terminal station of suffering but as a junction leading to a new course. A trajectory soaked in the strength of resilience, decorated with unprecedented personal growth, and dominated by a refreshed purpose that drives meaning in your life. By shifting your perspective, you can turn the adversities of your past into the architecture of your future, building a life marked by trauma but defined by purpose and growth.

Infusing purpose into life after trauma is no less than a rebirth. In this journey, you are born anew — born out of trials, tribulations, and the sheer will to endure. And most importantly, born with an elevated sense of purpose that you have sculpted out of your adversities.

Chapter 10. Building Resilience: Strategies and Techniques

Resilience is not merely our capacity to bounce back from adversity; it is also our proactive strength to confront future adversaries with a honed spirit. Fortunately, resilience is not a fixed trait; it can be built and cemented into our beings. Several strategies and techniques can help foster this indispensable quality, enabling us to encounter trials and tribulations with a robust and unwavering resolve.

10.1. Identifying Personal Strengths

Every individual possesses a unique set of strengths, visible or latent, which can contribute vitally towards building resilience. These strengths might be intellectual, such as analytical thinking or problem-solving, or they might be character strengths like empathy, determination, or gratitude. The key is to recognize and appreciate these strengths, and employ them proactively in the face of adversity.

Awareness of one's strengths can be amplified through self-reflection and introspection. Posing reflective questions and journaling the answers, you can draw out concealed personal strengths. You might also consider seeking feedback from people you trust—those who can provide an honest evaluation about your strong suits.

10.2. Cultivating Optimism

A positive mindset plays an important role in fostering resilience. An optimistic perspective allows us to view adversities not as life-defeating catastrophes, but as opportunities for growth and learning. This mindset does not negate or dismiss the existence of hardships, but redefines them to serve as stepping-stones rather than stumbling blocks.

Several strategies help in developing optimism. One is practicing gratitude — dedicating time each day to acknowledge the positive aspects of life, be they minor or major. Positive affirmations, mental visualizations of positive outcomes, and mindfully focusing on positive aspects rather than dwelling solely on negative aspects, can also foster an optimistic outlook.

10.3. Enhancing Social Connections

Social connectedness can provide essential emotional and practical support during difficult times. Therefore, investing time and effort in nurturing relationships is a valuable resilience-building strategy.

Connecting with others doesn't necessarily mean having a vast social network. It can translate into deepening existing relationships, seeking out new people who share similar interests, or pursuing opportunities where helping others allows you to build relationships.

10.4. Embracing Change

Resistance to change can increase the feeling of vulnerability in turbulent times, thus depleting resilience. On the other hand, embracing change can enhance acceptance and adaptability, important facets of resilience.

Accepting that life is laden with changes and unpredictability can be achieved by developing flexibility and adaptability. Flexibility refers to the capacity to adjust thoughts and actions according to changing situations. Adaptability, meanwhile, refers to proactively preparing for potential changes or challenges.

10.5. Building Emotional Intelligence

Emotional intelligence (EI) is the capacity to understand and regulate one's emotions, simultaneously tuning into others' emotions. High EI can help you cope with emotional distress, preventing it from overwhelming your patience and resilience.

Building EI can be achieved through self-reflection, mindfulness practices, and seeking constructive feedback on how you manage emotions. Empathy and active listening can help develop an understanding of others' emotional states.

10.6. Practicing Mindfulness and Self-care

Mindfulness - being in the present moment, coupled with self-care - looking after one's physical, emotional, and mental well-being, can be potent resilience-enhancing strategies.

Mindfulness exercises, such as meditation, deep-breathing, guided imagery, or yoga, promote a sense of calm and focus. Coupled with self-care practices like regular physical activity, balanced nutrition, sufficient sleep, and prioritized leisure time, these techniques can significantly reinforce resilience.

10.7. Seeking Professional Help

It can be beneficial to seek professional support in the journey to build resilience. Mental health professionals can provide tools and techniques to recognize negative thinking patterns, develop coping strategies, and bolster confidence. Therapy groups offer an environment where individuals can learn from each other's experiences and build supportive networks.

Resilience is one of the keystones that allows us to turn adversities into avenues of growth. By using the aforementioned strategies and techniques, the journey through life's challenging terrains can be navigated with greater power, poise, and confidence. Not only can we survive the storms we encounter, but we can also emerge from them stronger and more enriched.

Chapter 11. Post-Traumatic Growth: A New Beginning

When the tsunami of trauma threatens to erode the shores of our emotional resilience, it can seem as though life will never be the same again. However, instead of being drowned, many survivors learn not just to float but to swim to newer shores of inner strength and growth. This intriguing process yields the unique gemstone that we call Post-Traumatic Growth (PTG).

11.1. Understanding Post-Traumatic Growth

Post-Traumatic Growth is a positive psychological change experienced as a result of adversity and other challenges, which leads to a higher level of functioning. Rather than merely bouncing back, PTG sees individuals bouncing forward, achieving a transformative alteration of their life outlook following their adversity. PTG encapsulates changes in three broad domains: changes in self-perception, changes in interpersonal relationships, and changes in philosophy of life.

11.2. Paving the Path to PTG: Self-Perception

Self-perception entails an individual's perception of their personal strengths as well as consequent self-esteem. People enduring trauma often report increased recognition of their inner strength. Post-trauma, they not only feel more in control, but also develop a deeper understanding of their potential and capabilities.

This metamorphosis in self-perception often fosters higher self-esteem and self-confidence. By enduring adverse experiences, individuals tend to understand the depth of their resilience. This can impact their self-efficacy, enabling them to believe in their abilities to overcome future obstacles and adversities.

11.3. Altering Interpersonal Relationships

The road to PTG also sees significant modifications in one's interpersonal relationships. The experience can deepen existing social ties as people realize the importance and potency of social support. They might appreciate their relationships more, investing greater time and emotions in nurturing them.

Rejuvenated relationships do not merely involve the strengthening of old bonds but also the forging of new ones. Shared adversities or support groups can lead to new friendships, fostering a sense of belonging, connection, and understanding — elements crucial to healing and growth.

11.4. Philosophy of Life: A Shift in Perspective

Lastly, PTG imbues survivors with a refurbished philosophy of life. This can manifest as a greater appreciation for life and a shift in life priorities. The individual might become more present, appreciating the impermanence of life and the beauty in each passing moment.

Often, survivors learn to find joy in small things, cultivating gratitude in their daily lives. Further, the shift in perspective often brings a redirection of life's goals and aspirations. People who experience PTG might find newer meaning in life, sometimes changing their entire career paths to align with this newfound purpose.

11.5. Facilitating PTG: Strategies and Steps

Mental flexibility is integral to PTG. It allows one to accept the changes brought about by the traumatic event and adjust accordingly. Grounded in cognitive reconstructing, it nudges individuals to view their adversities in a new light, enabling the reframing of the traumatic experience into a catalyst for growth.

Emotional regulation is equally vital. The ability to identify, understand, and manage one's emotional responses to traumatic stress can foster PTG, providing emotional stability. Additionally, the generation of positive emotions can serve as a buffer against the negative psychological effects of trauma.

Lastly, social support acts as a lighthouse guiding the survivors out of their tempestuous sea of adversities. Surrounding oneself with compassionate and understanding social networks can act as a vital bolster to psychological resilience, engendering hope and reducing feelings of loneliness and isolation.

11.6. PTG: The Pheonix Rises

Yes, trauma can shatter us. It can feel like a violent storm that leaves behind nothing but destruction and despair. Yet, from the ashes of such despair, the Phoenix of Post-Traumatic Growth arises. It imbues trauma survivors with a new sense of self, deepened relationships, and a revised philosophy of life.

It is this rebirth — this new beginning — that illuminates the path from trauma to transformation. By embracing the lessons found within pain, by rezoning hurt into healing, by rescripting rejection into redirection, individuals can breakthrough their bounds, discovering an empowered version of themselves — one resurgent, resilient, and reborn.

Like stretching the tightly strung bow to shoot the arrow further, adversities stretch our emotional and psychological capacities, plunging us into profound depths only to rise stronger, higher, and farther. This is the empowering journey of Post-Traumatic Growth, a testament to human resilience, a beacon of hope, and above all, a celebration of the indomitable human spirit.